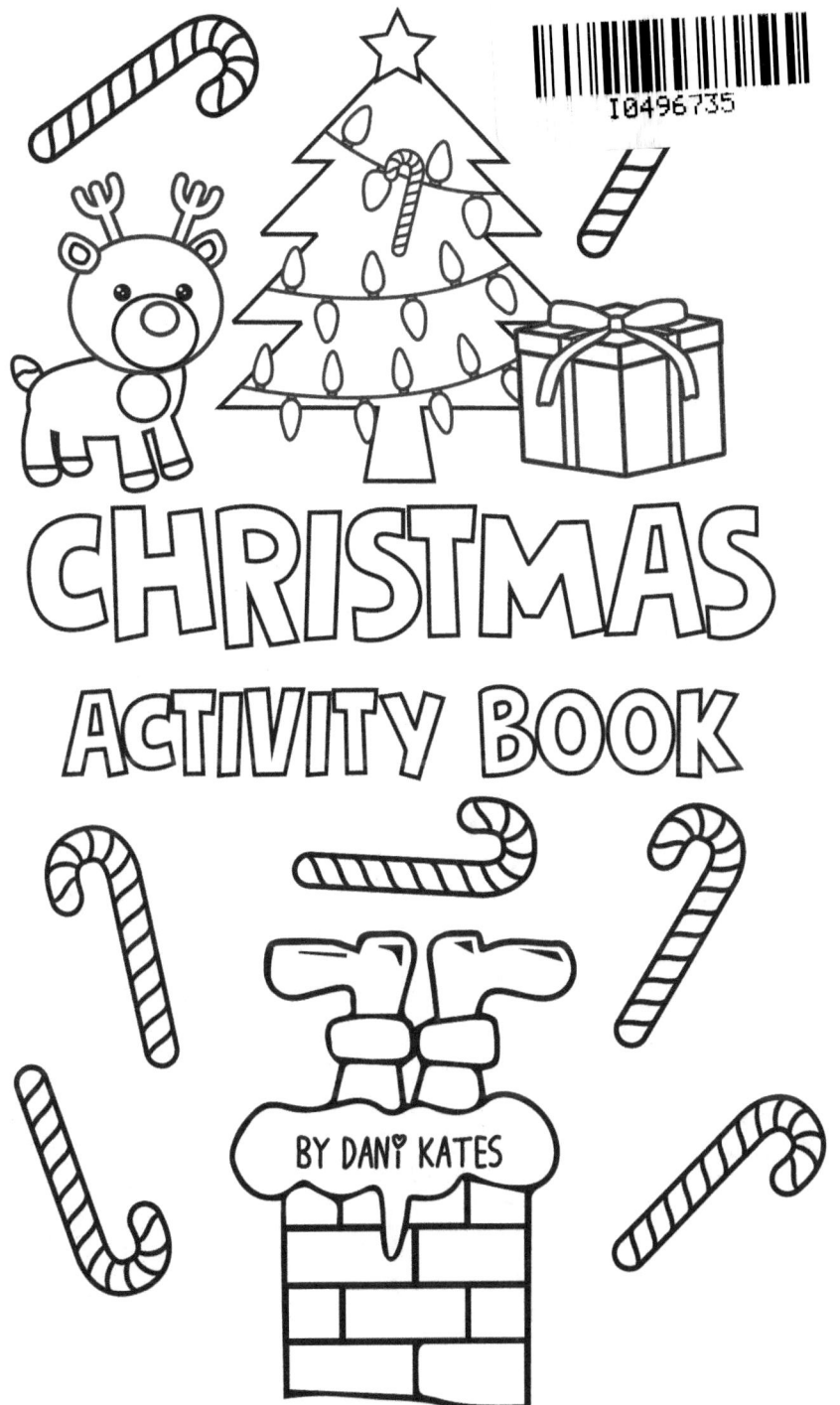

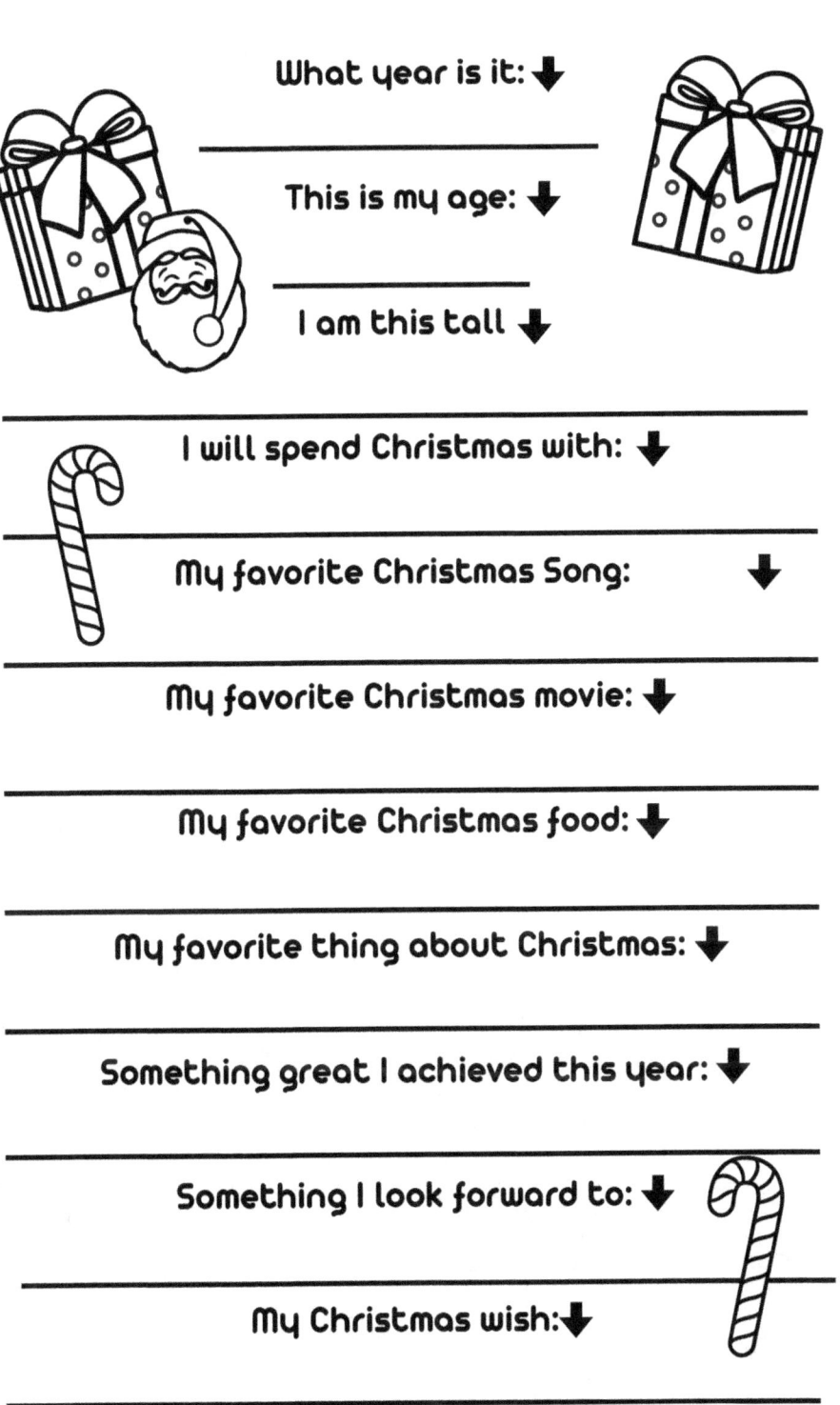

ONLY 2 OF THESE CHRISTMAS TREES ARE THE SAME. COLOR THEM ALL AND CIRCLE THOSE 2

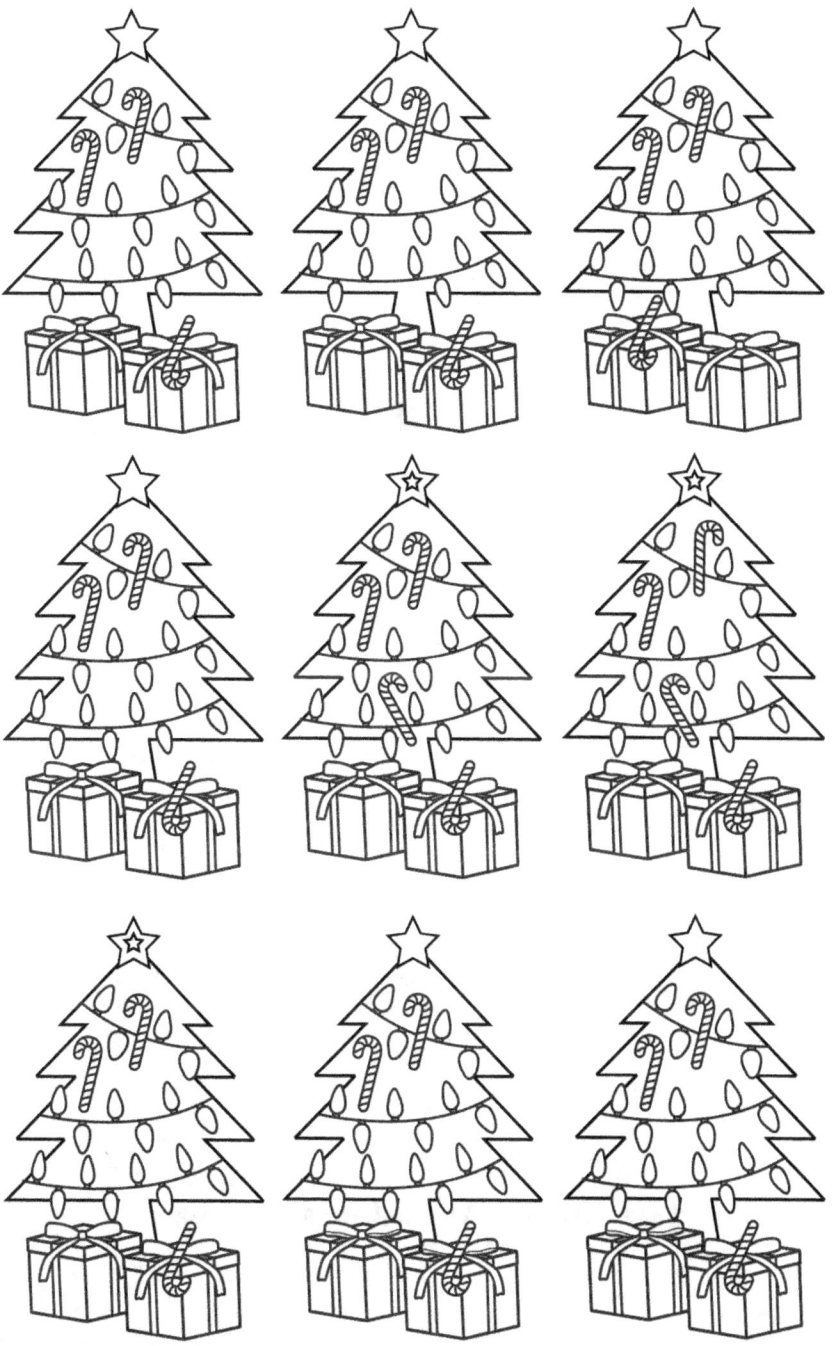

(the bottom row, 2nd and 3rd are the same)

Christmas Wordsearch

```
E F D C H S L E I G H R A A A
B Y X M F I G Q W C X P S E V
L I G H T S E I K O O C A I T
F U R M X N B L F P A H S B F
M K C X W Y I E T Z Z G O G G
G B C X S N O W M A N I I H I
B S A M T S I R H C X N E O F
Y L L O H T R P W I F G E R T
S J E K D Q E I Z E X E X N S
Y A A T C M I R O D I R W A N
S D N V S Z N E D N Y B O M D
Z X J T H K D P J M B R N E T
B V E L A N E N N G Y E S N E
B P V L R O E U F S G A T T R
Z M E C N T R F D R X D E X X
```

CHRISTMAS GINGERBREAD COOKIES
SANTA ORNAMENT SNOWMAN
REINDEER LIGHTS HOLLY
SNOW GIFTS SLEIGH

**ONLY 2 OF THESE TOY SOLDIERS ARE THE SAME.
COLORING THEM WILL HELP YOU FIGURE OUT WHICH 2 IT IS!**

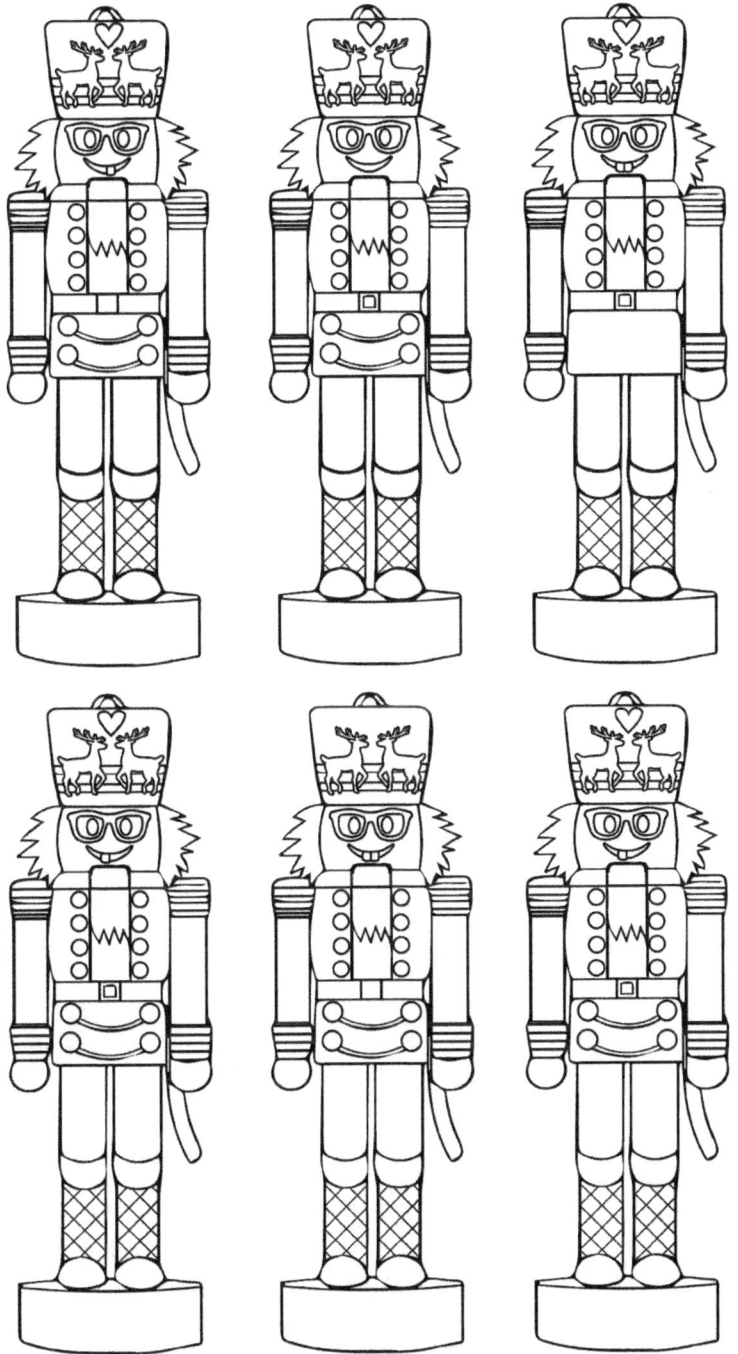

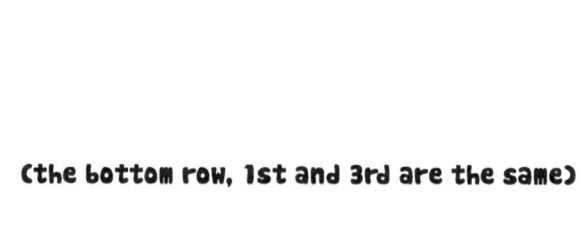

WORD FINDER

Find words using the letters in the words CHRISTMAS PRESENT. The letters in the words have to be touching (next to, above/below, or diagonal from eachother)

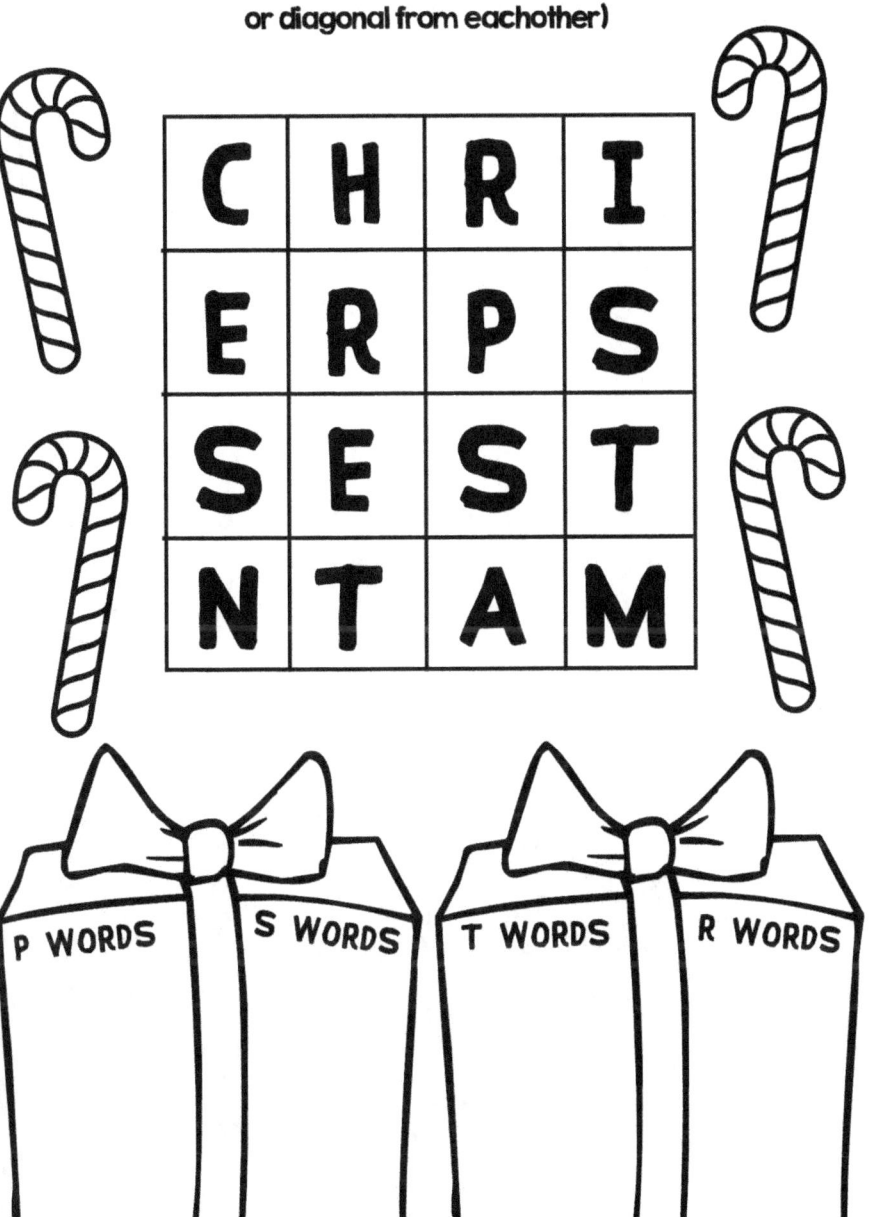

My Favorite Christmas Foods

1. _____
2. _____
3. _____
4. _____

My Favorite Christmas Songs

1. _____
2. _____
3. _____

My Favorite Christmas Movies

1. _____
2. _____
3. _____

ONLY TWO OF THESE SANTAS ARE THE SAME. COLOR THEM ALL AND FIND THOSE 2

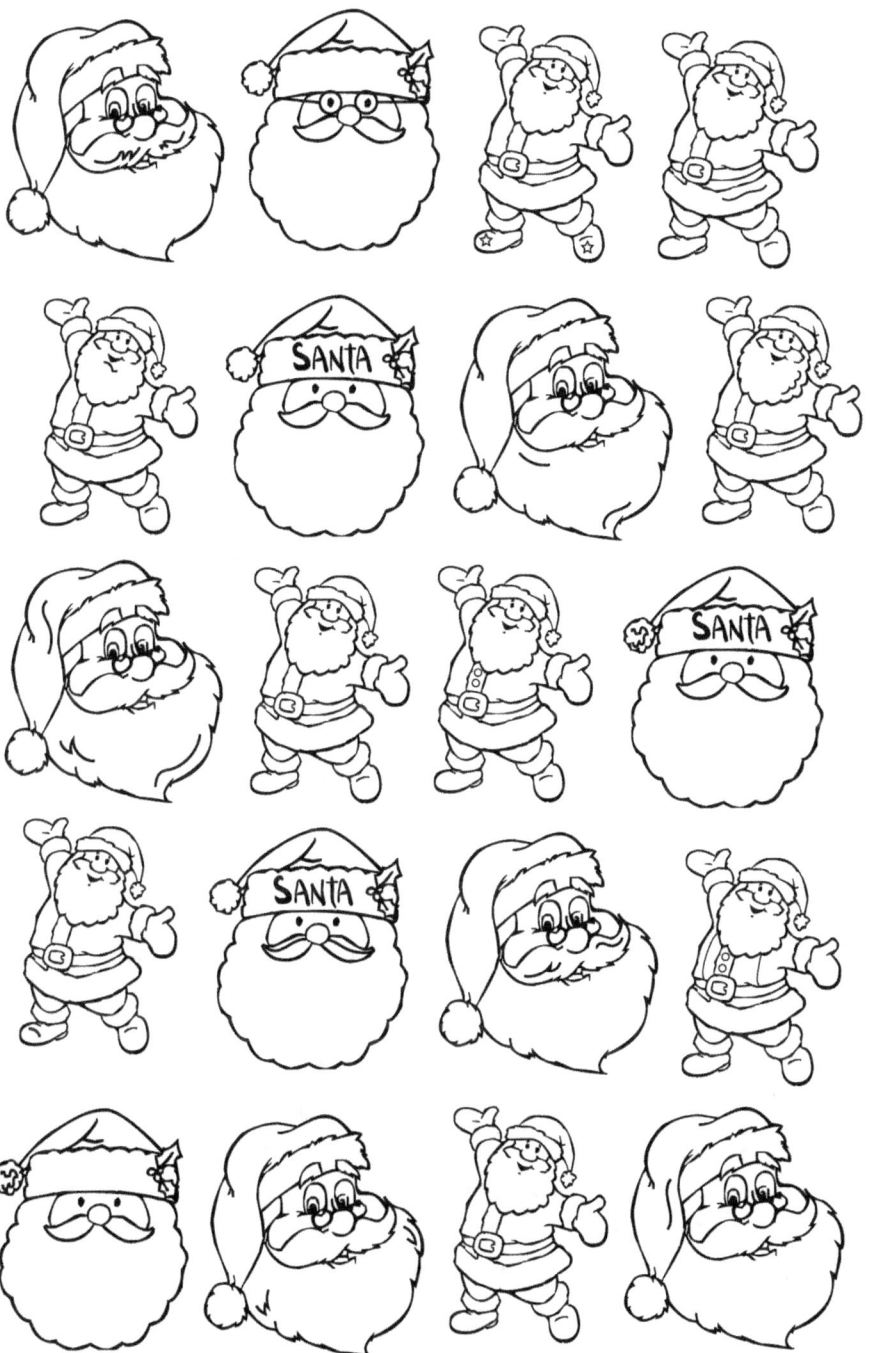

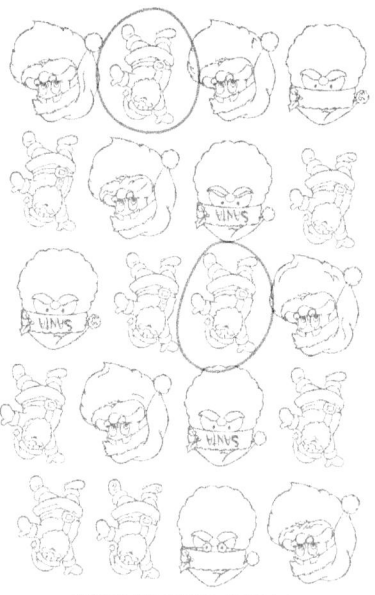

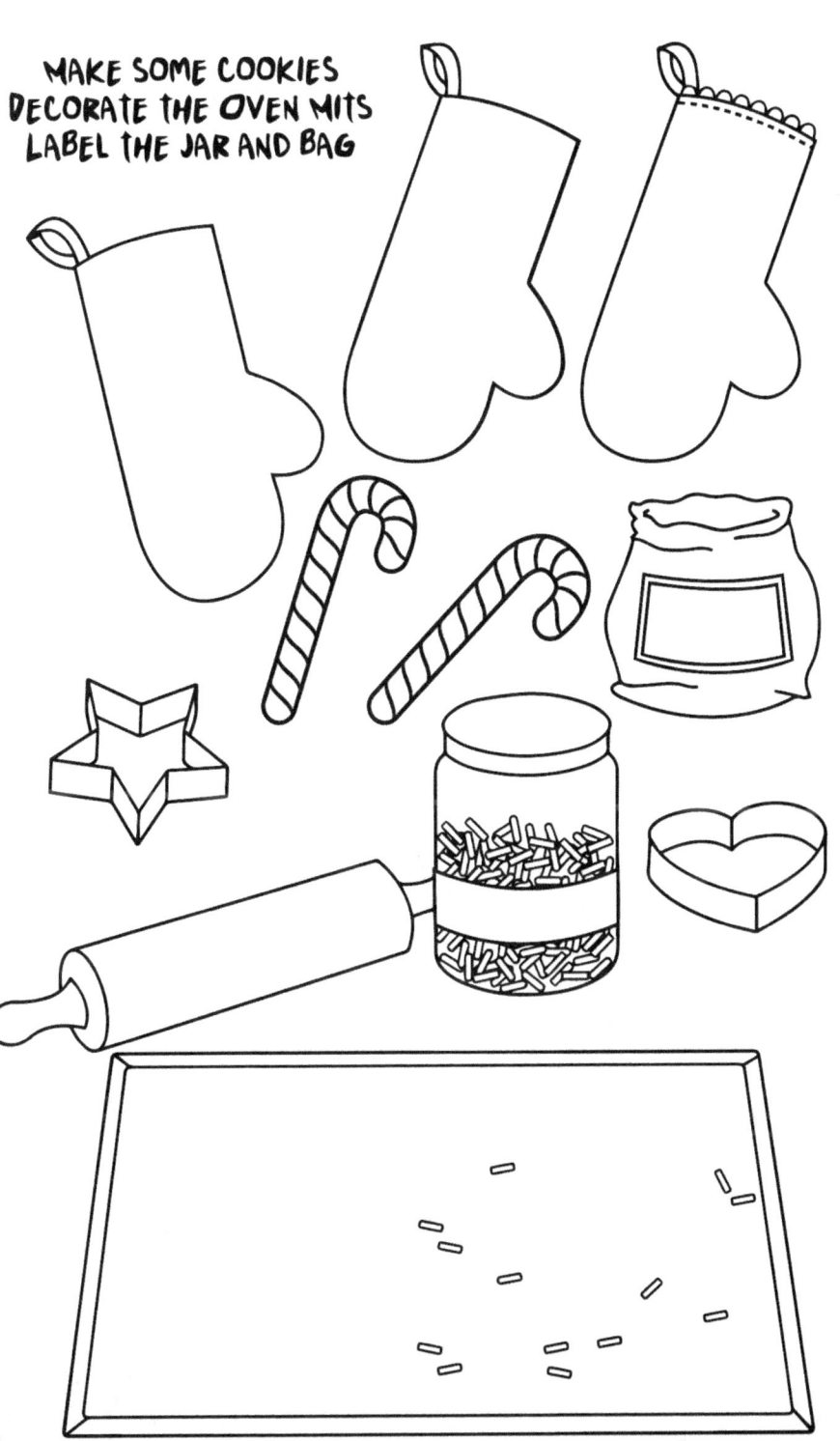

BRING THE GIFTS TO THE TREE THRU THE MAZE

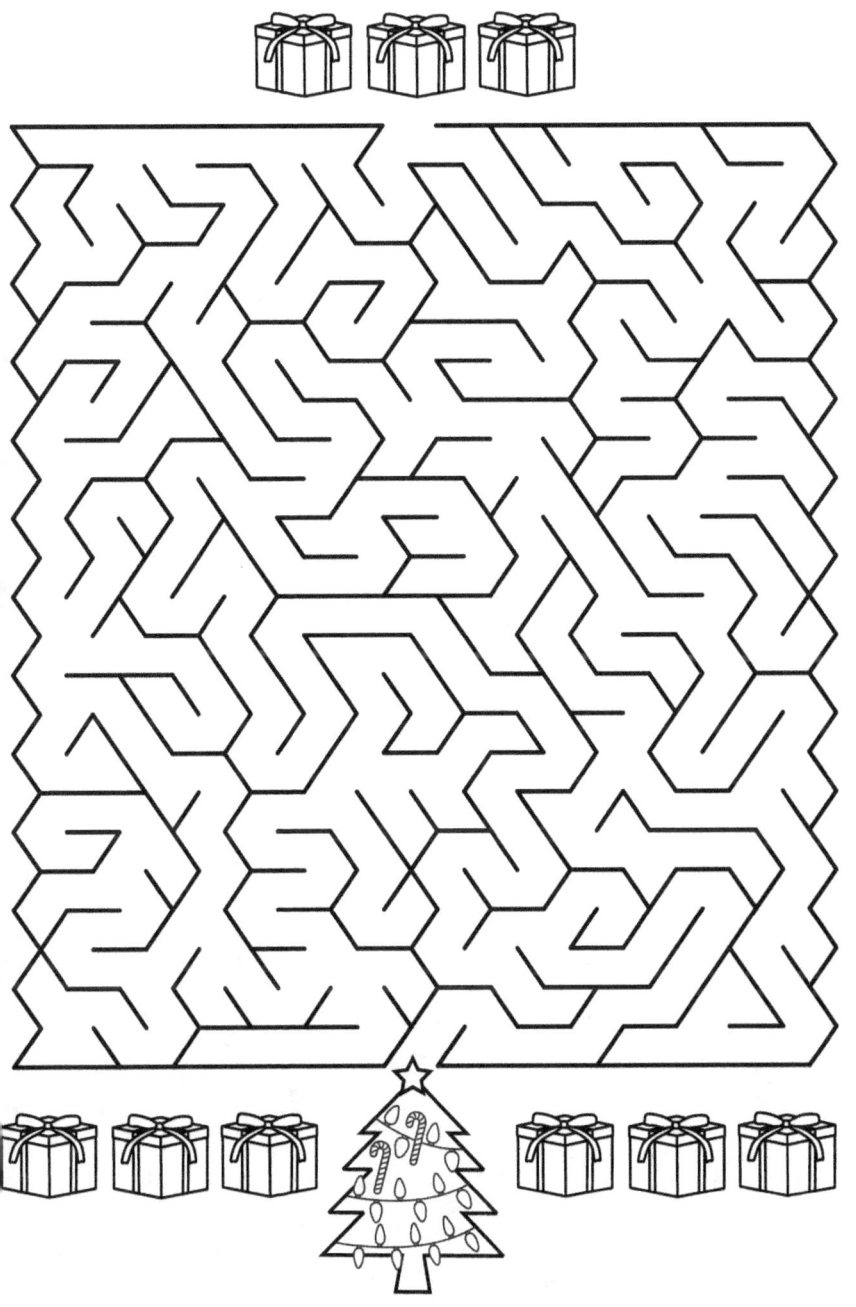

WHAT IS YOUR CHRISTMAS NAME?

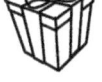 ## First Letter of Your First Name: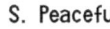

A. Jolly	J. Magical	S. Peaceful
B. Happy	K. Snowy	T. Frosty
C. Merry	L. Glittery	U. Sugary
D. Wonderful	M. Magnificent	V. Cheerful
E. White	N. Super	W. Sweet
F. Excitable	O. Sparkly	X. Remarkable
G. Delicious	P. Fantastical	Y. Traditional
H. Fantastic	Q. Memorable	Z. Splendid
I. Great	R. Beautiful	

First Letter of Your Last Name:

A. Cinnamon	J. Sugarplum	S. Caramel
B. Marshmallow	K. Twinkle	T. Candy Cane
C. Chocolate	L. Honey	U. Sprinkle
D. Gingerbread	M. Snickerdoodle	V. Ribbon
E. Holiday	N. Tinsel	W. Pixie
F. Festive	O. Peppermint	X. Ginger
G. Nutmeg	P. Minty	Y. Twinkly
H. Marshmallow	Q. Angel	Z. Berry
I. Chocolate	R. Coconut	

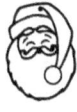 Your Birth Month:

January: Claus	May: Tree	September: Ornament
February: Reindeer	June: Present	October: Mistletoe
March: Elf	July: Stocking	November: Sleigh
April: Snowman	August: Bells	December: Cookie

MY CHRISTMAS FRIENDS + FAMILY

Using the Christmas Name Generator from the previous page, make a list of your family friends!

NAME	CHRISTMAS NAME

CHRISTMAS WISHES

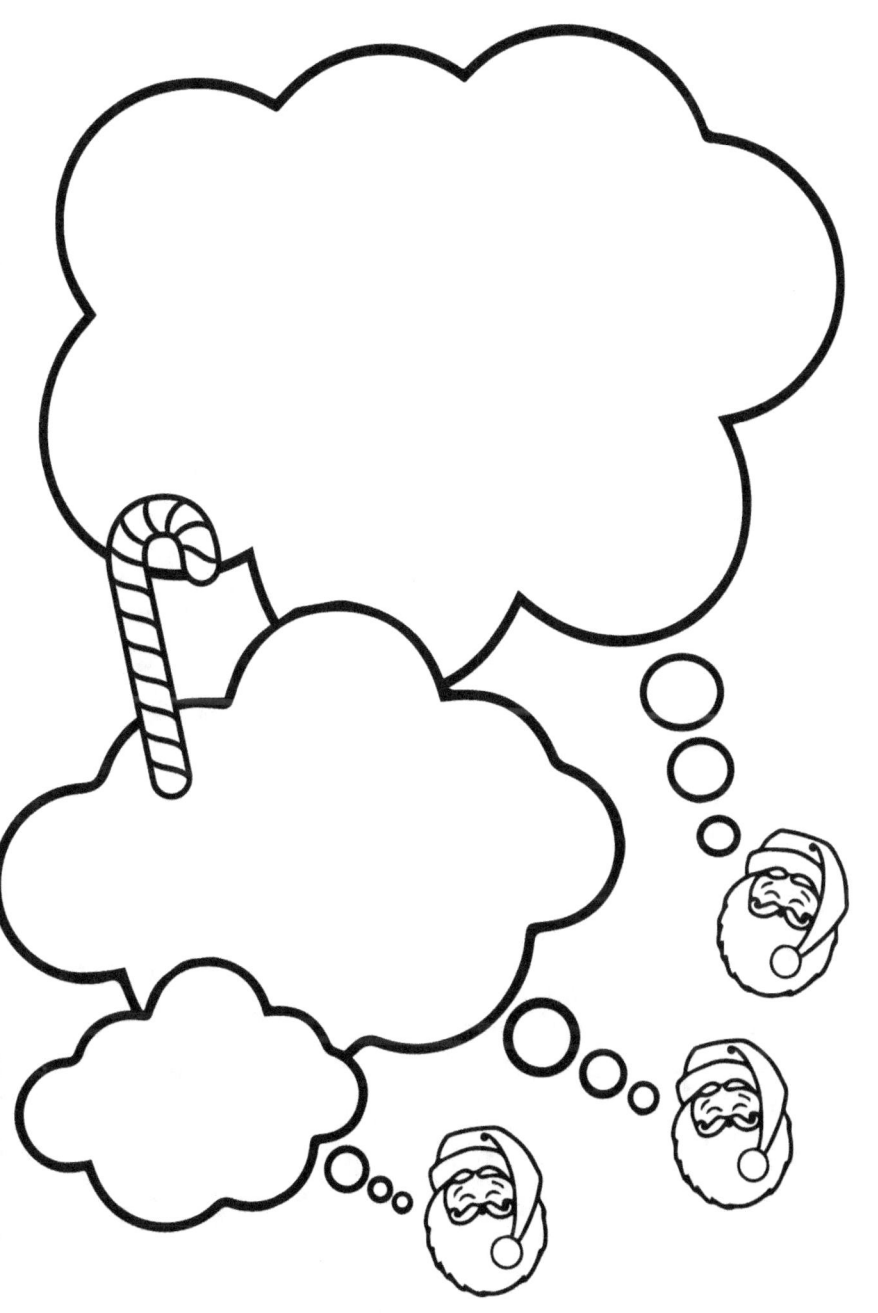

CHRISTMAS GIFTS FOR YOU!

WHAT IS INSIDE EACH BOX? LABEL THEM ALL. THEN DESIGN SOME CHRISTMAS WRAPPING PAPER FOR THEM.

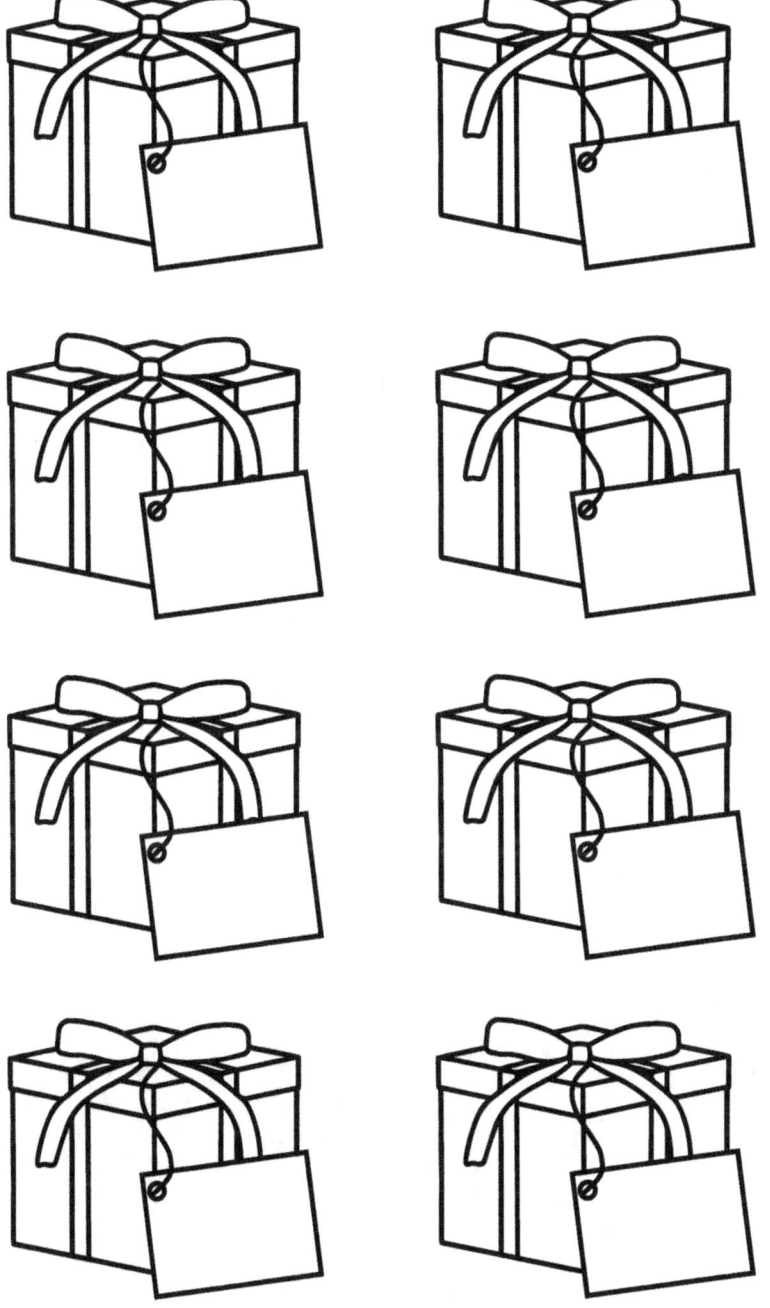

TO:

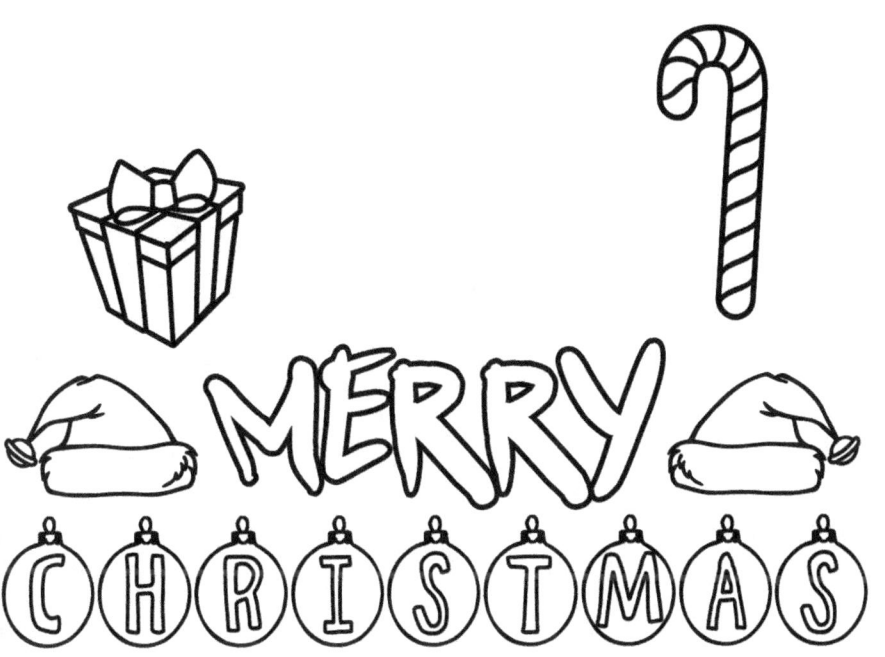

LOVE:

if you were planning a...

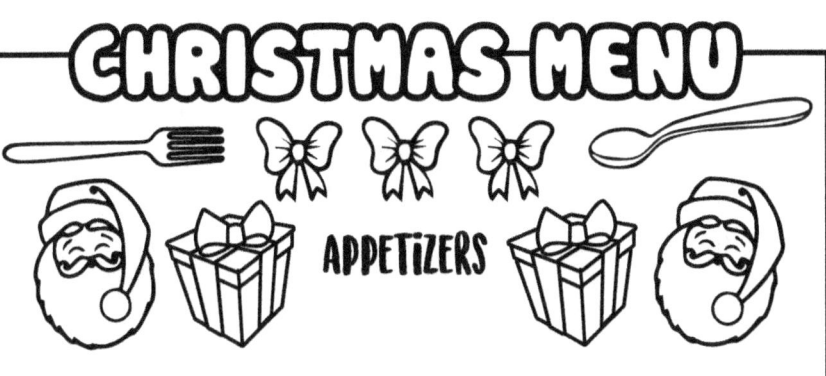

APPETIZERS

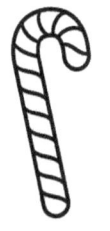

MAIN DISHES

SIDE DISHES

DESSERTS

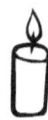
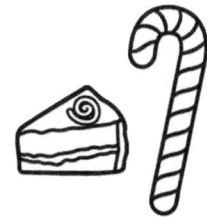

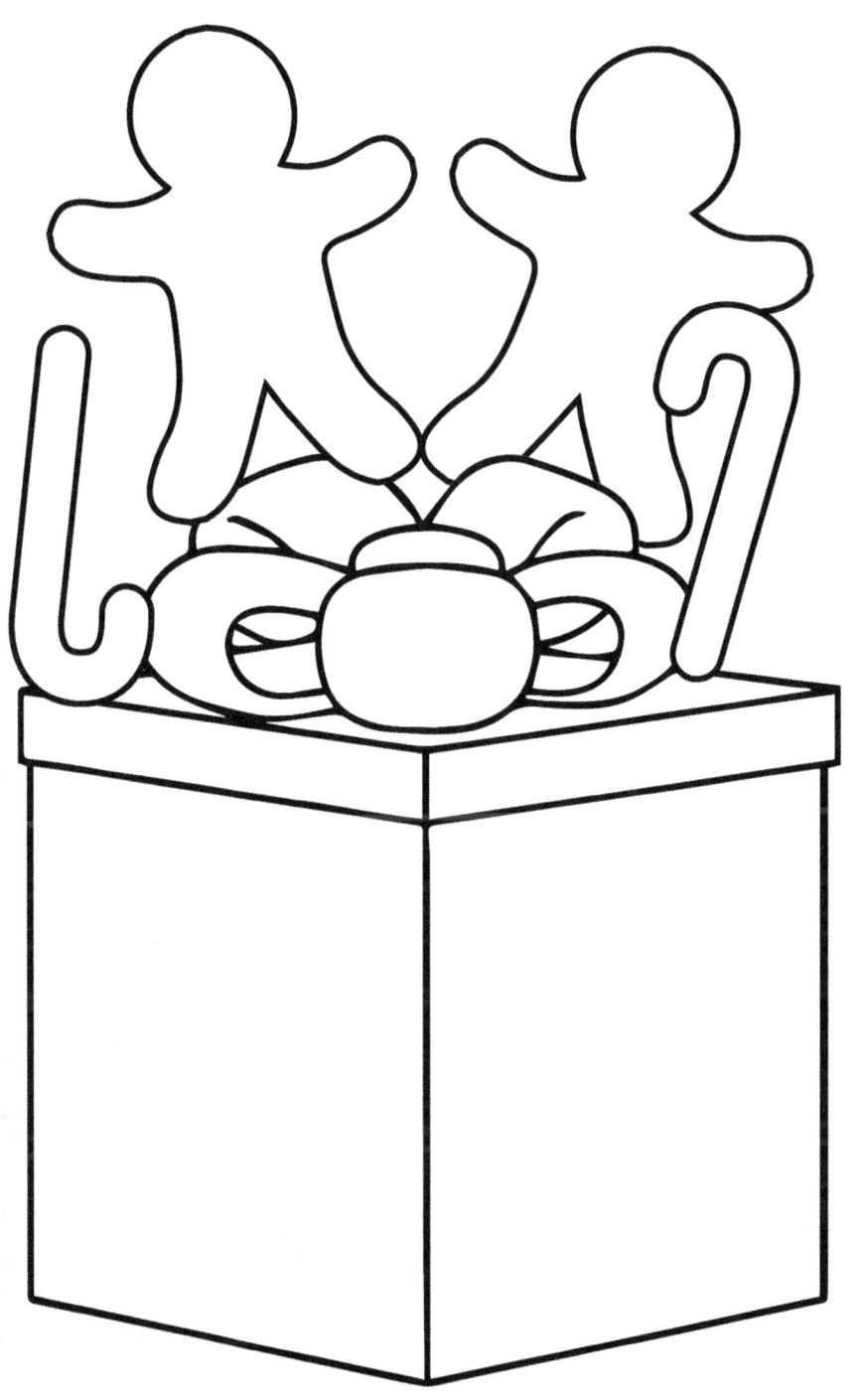

DECORATE THE GIFT, CANDY CANES, & GINGERBREAD MEN

🎵 Christmas songs 🎵

santa claus is _ _ _ _ _ _ _ to _ _ _ _ _.

🎵 _ _ _ _ _ _ christmas 🎵

🎵 all i _ _ _ _ for christmas 🎵

🎵 Rockin' _ _ _ _ _ _ _ the tree 🎵
_ _ _ _ _ _ _ _ _ _ _

i saw mommy _ _ _ _ _ _ _
_ _ _ _ _ _ _ _ _

its beginning to _ _ _ _ _ a lot _ _ _ _ _
🎵 christmas

_ _ _ _ _ _ _ bells

Run _ _ _ _ _ _ _ _ Run

baby, it's _ _ _ _ _ _ _ _ _ _ _ _.

_ _ _ _ _ _ _ night 🎵

Santa Claus is coming to town
White Christmas
All I want for Christmas
Rockin' around the Christmas tree
I saw mommy kissing Santa Claus
It's beginning to look a lot like Christmas
Jingle Bells
Run Rudolph Run
Baby it's Cold Outside
Silent night

color the snowmen and find the only 2 that are the same

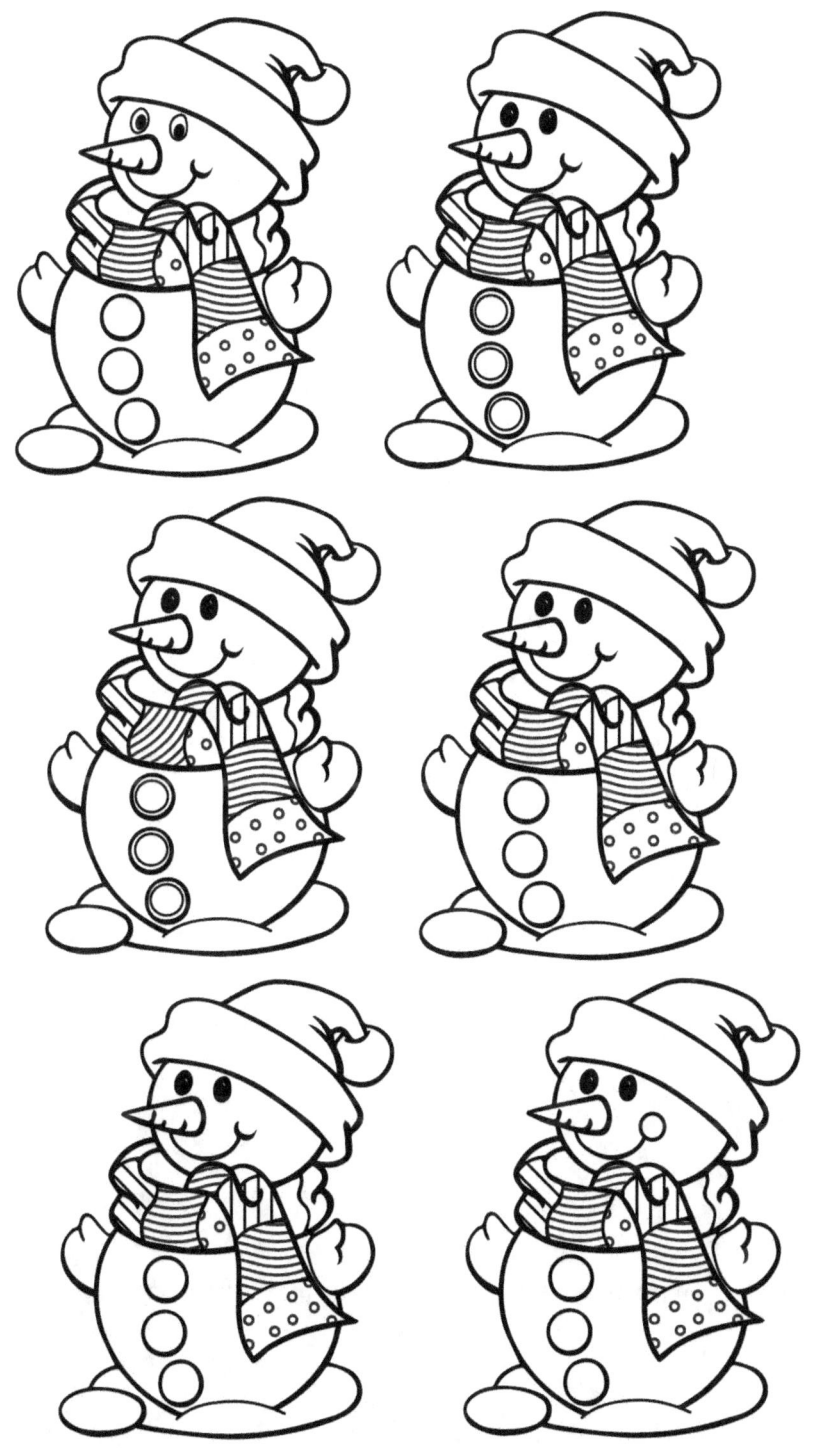

MIDDLE RIGHT AND BOTTOM LEFT ARE THE SAME

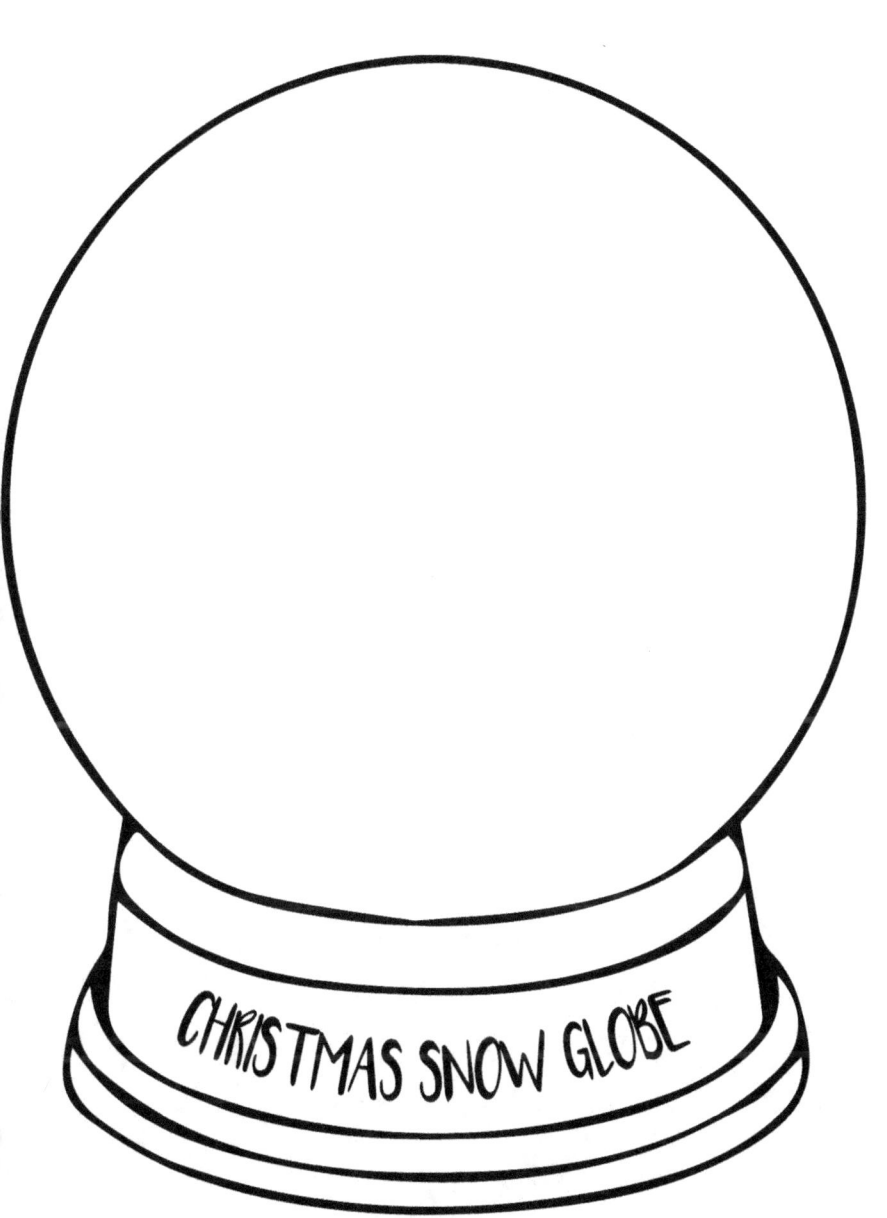

**USE THE FIRST LETTER OF EACH LINE
TO WRITE A POEM OR STORY ABOUT CHRISTMAS**

C _____

H _____

R _____

I _____

S _____

T _____

M _____

A _____

S _____

Soft Christmas Cookies

INGREDIENTS

3 3/4 CUPS ALL-PURPOSE FLOUR
1 TEASPOON BAKING POWDER
1/2 TEASPOON SALT
1 CUP MARGARINE, SOFTENED
1 1/2 CUPS WHITE SUGAR
2 EGGS
2 TEASPOONS VANILLA EXTRACT

SPRINKLES, FROSTING, CANDY FOR DECORATING

DIRECTIONS

SIFT FLOUR, BAKING POWDER, & SALT TOGETHER, SET ASIDE. IN A LARGE BOWL, CREAM TOGETHER THE MARGARINE & SUGAR UNTIL LIGHT & FLUFFY.

BEAT IN THE EGGS ONE AT A TIME, THEN STIR IN THE VANILLA. GRADUALLY BLEND IN THE SIFTED INGREDIENTS UNTIL FULLY ABSORBED. COVER DOUGH, AND CHILL FOR 2 HOURS.

PREHEAT OVEN TO 400 DEGREES F. GREASE COOKIE SHEETS. IN A CLEAN FLOURED SURFACE, ROLL OUT SMALL PORTIONS OF CHILLED DOUGH TO 1/4 INCH THICKNESS. CUT OUT SHAPES USING COOKIE CUTTERS.

BAKE 6 TO 8 MINUTES IN THE PREHEATED OVEN, OR UNTIL EDGES ARE BARELY BROWN. REMOVE FROM COOKIE SHEETS TO COOL ON WIRE RACKS.

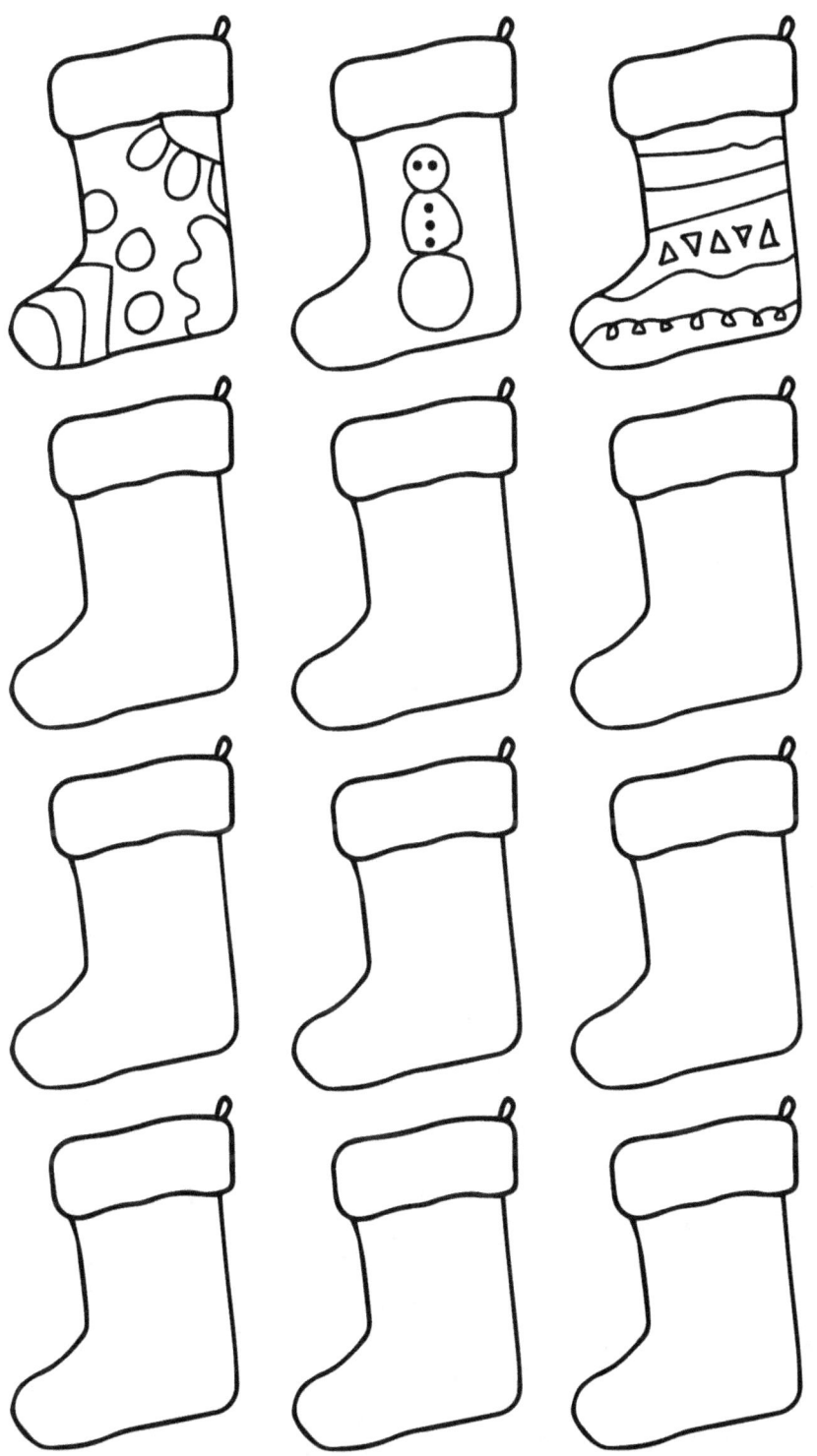

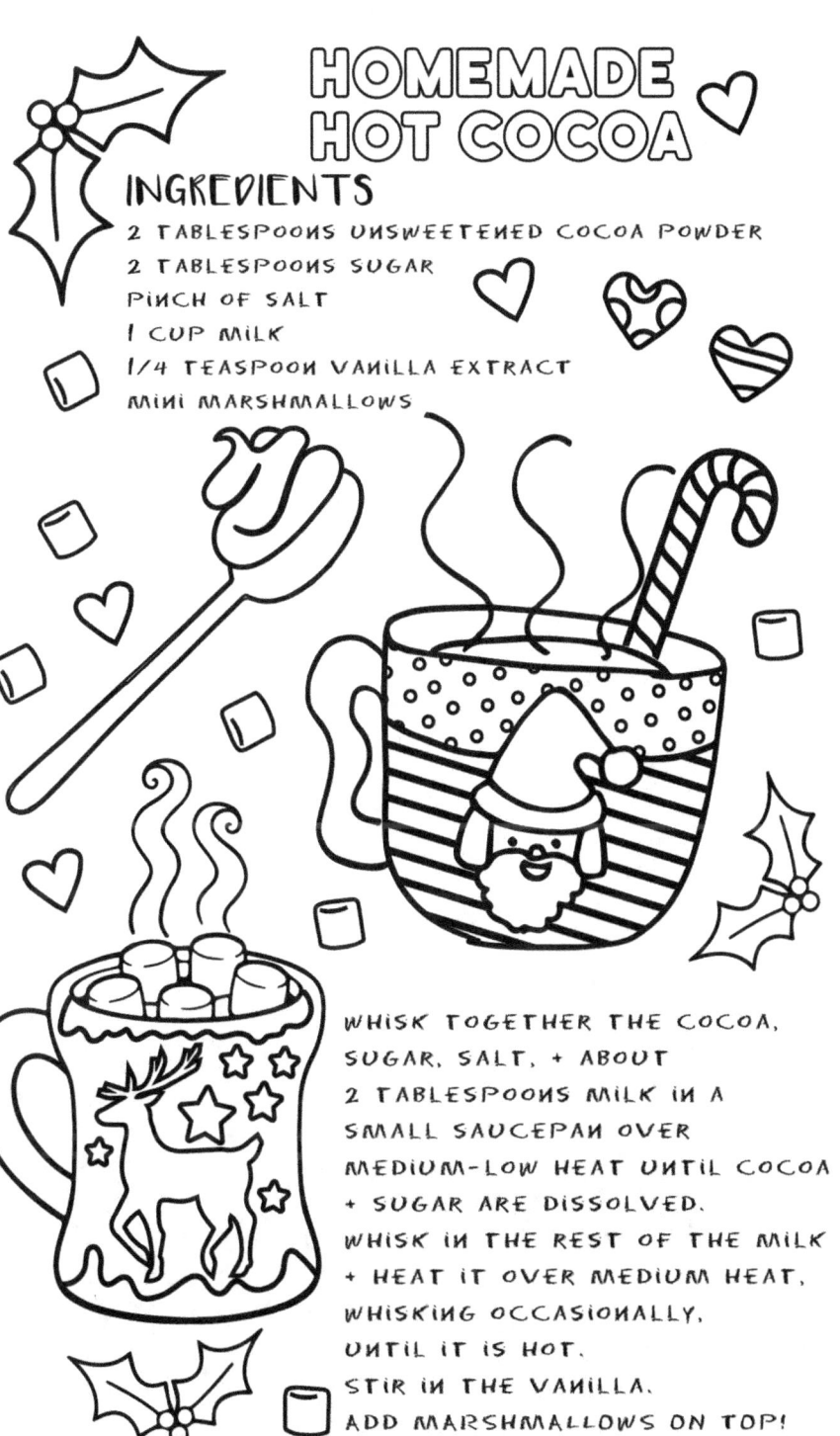

DECORATE THE CHRISTMAS TREE AND GIFTS!

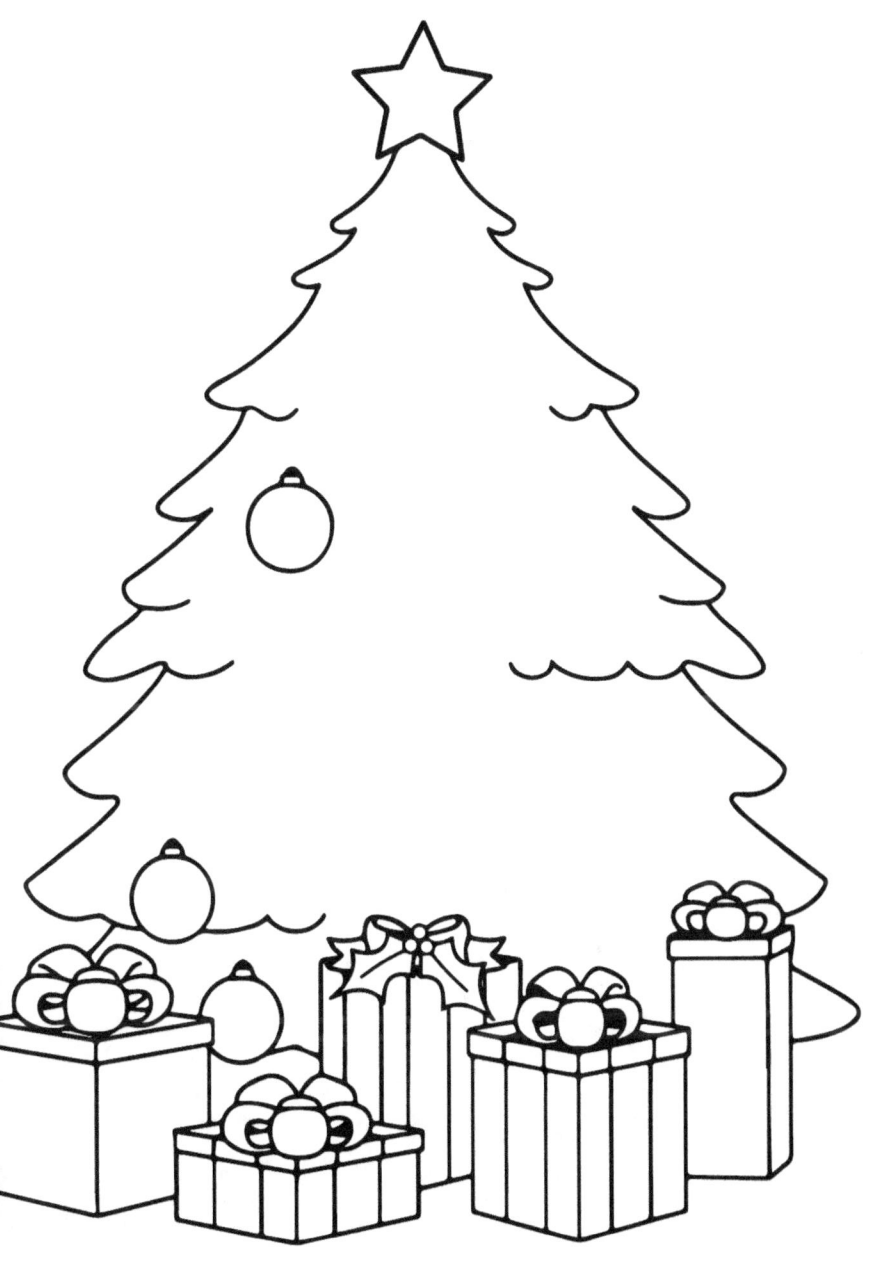

PUT SOME LIGHTS ON THESE WIRES

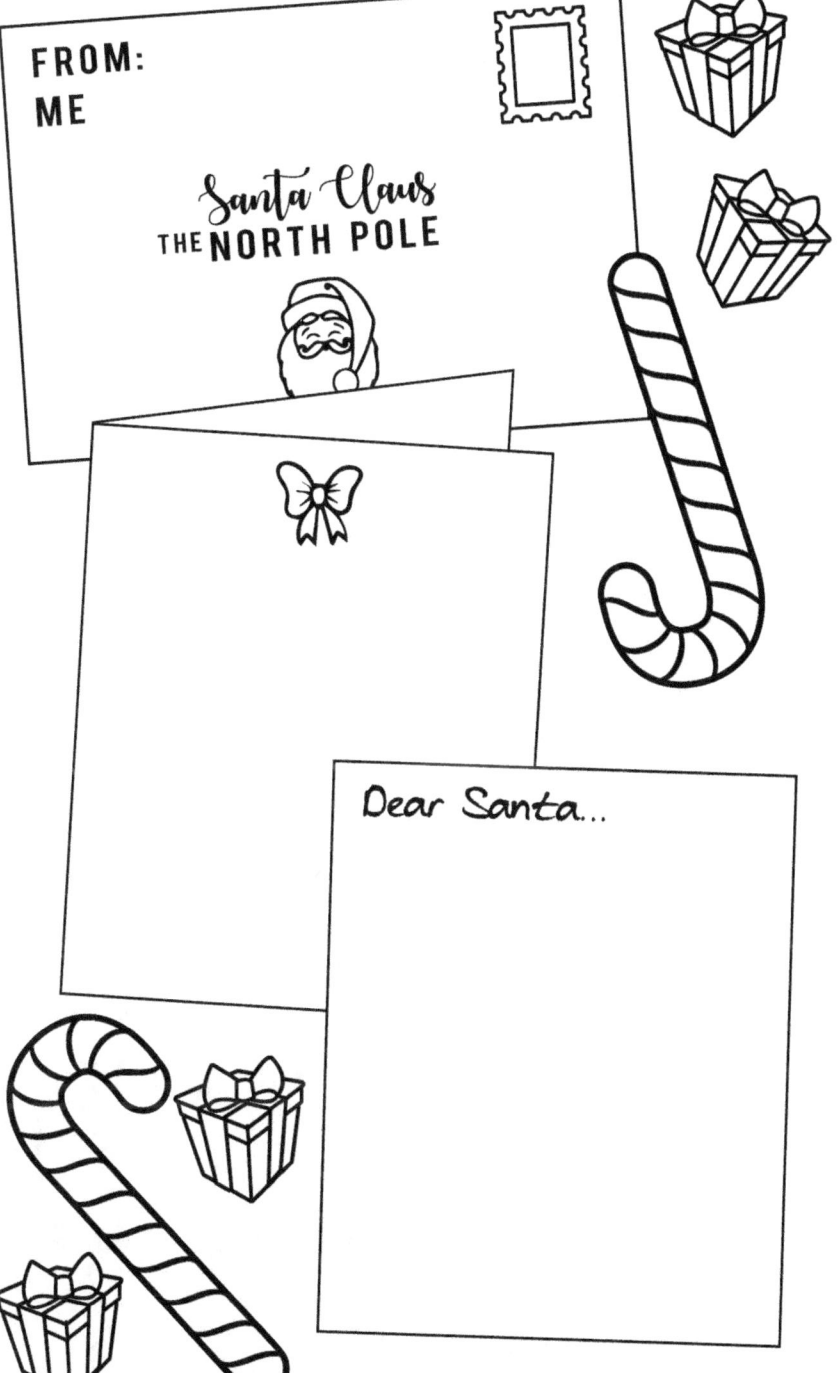

DECORATE A GINGERBREAD HOUSE.

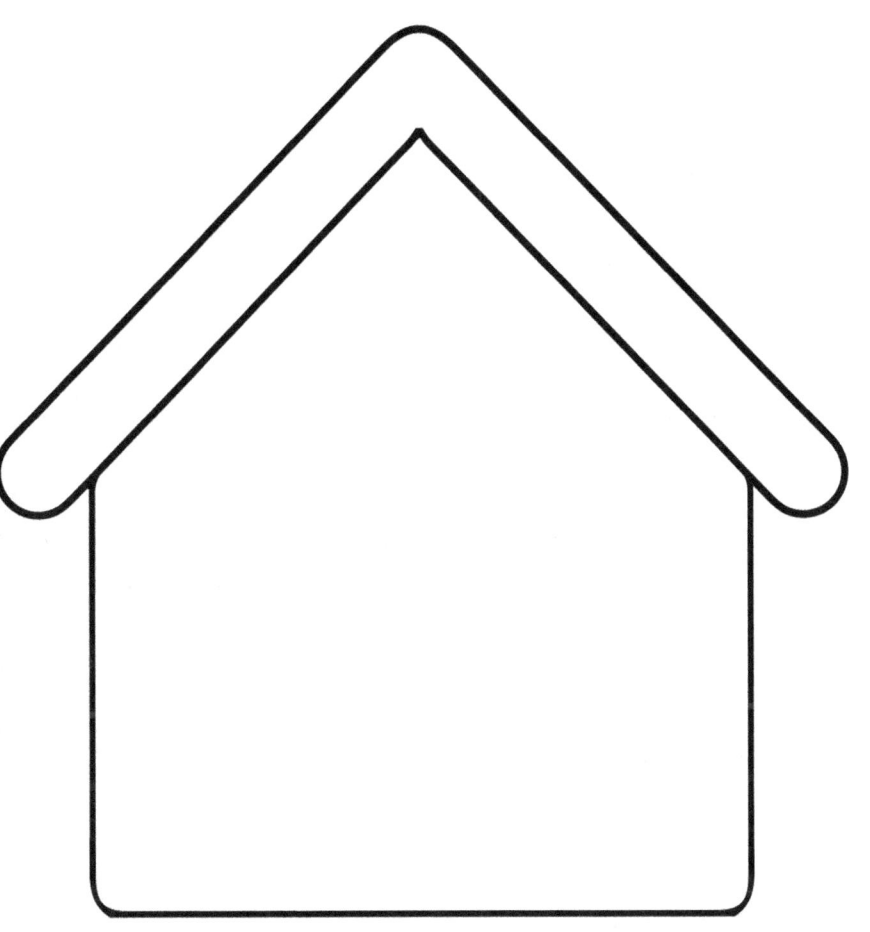

THE THINGS I LOVE ABOUT CHRISTMAS

1. _____

2. _____

3. _____

4. _____

5. _____

6. _____

7. _____

8. _____

9. _____

10. _____

Christmas Trivia Questions

1. In the song "Frosty the Snowman," what made Frosty come to life?

 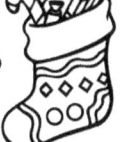

2. What Christmas beverage is also known as "milk punch"?

3. One of Santa's reindeer shares a name with a famous symbol of Valentine's Day. Which reindeer is that?

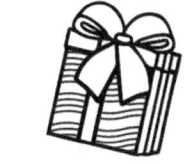 

4. Name all of santa's reindeer.

5. What Christmas-themed ballet premiered in Saint Petersburg, Russia in 1892?

6. In the song "Grandma Got Run Over by a Reindeer," what "incriminating" evidence was found on Grandma's back?

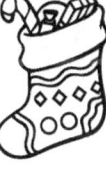 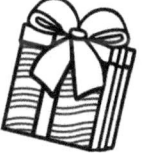

7. What was Scrooge's first name?

8. In frosty the snowman, who brought frosty back to life?

9. What were frosty's eyes made out of?

10. According to the song, what did my true love give to me on the 4th day of Christmas?

(answers on the back, no peeking!)

1. An old silk hat
2. Egg nog
3. Cupid
4. Dasher, Dancer, Prancer, Vixen, Comet, Cupid, Donner, Blitzen, Rudolph
5. The Nutcracker
6. Santa Claus marks
7. Ebenezer
8. Santa Claus
9. Coal
10. 4 calling birds

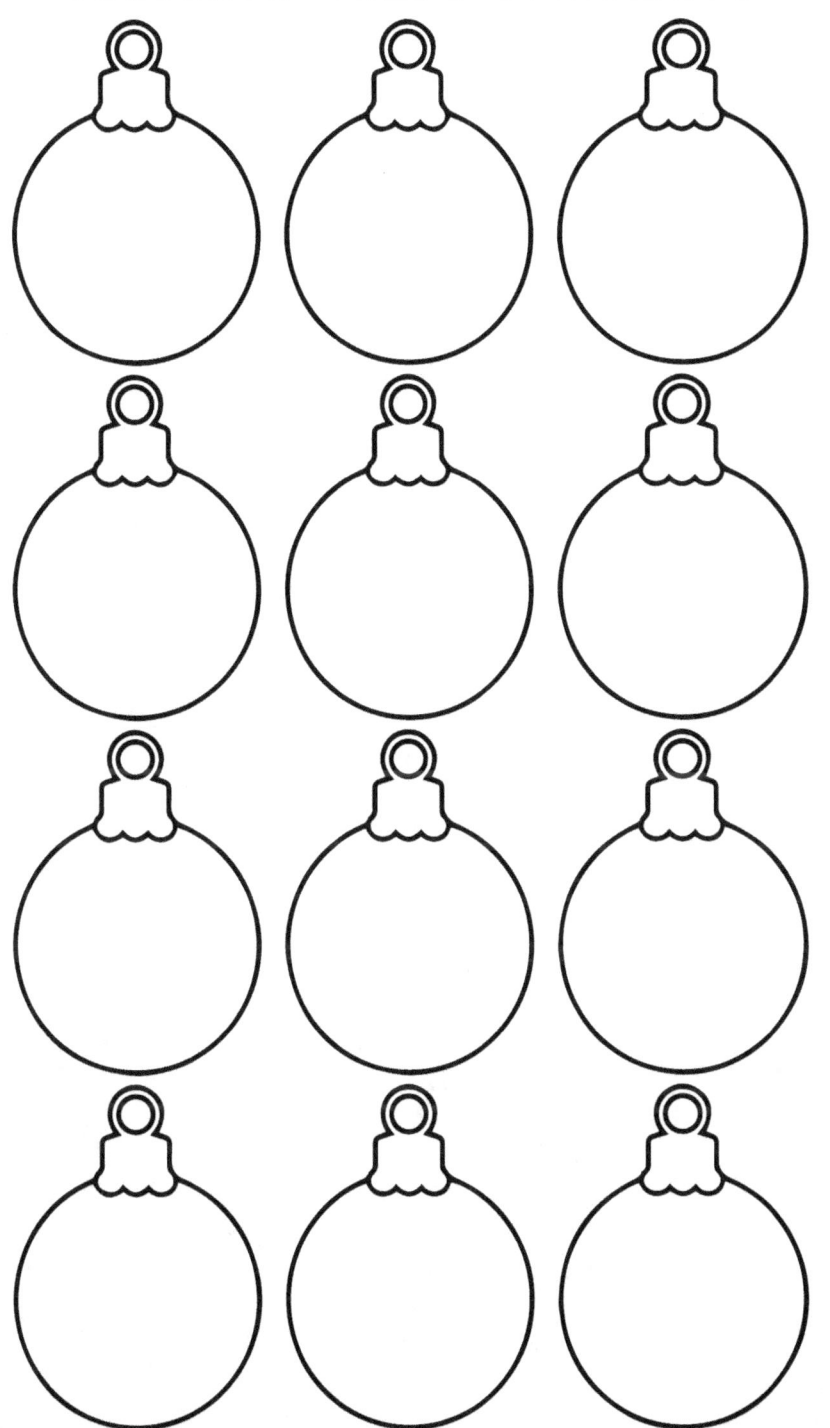

DESIGN AN UGLY CHRISTMAS SWEATER!

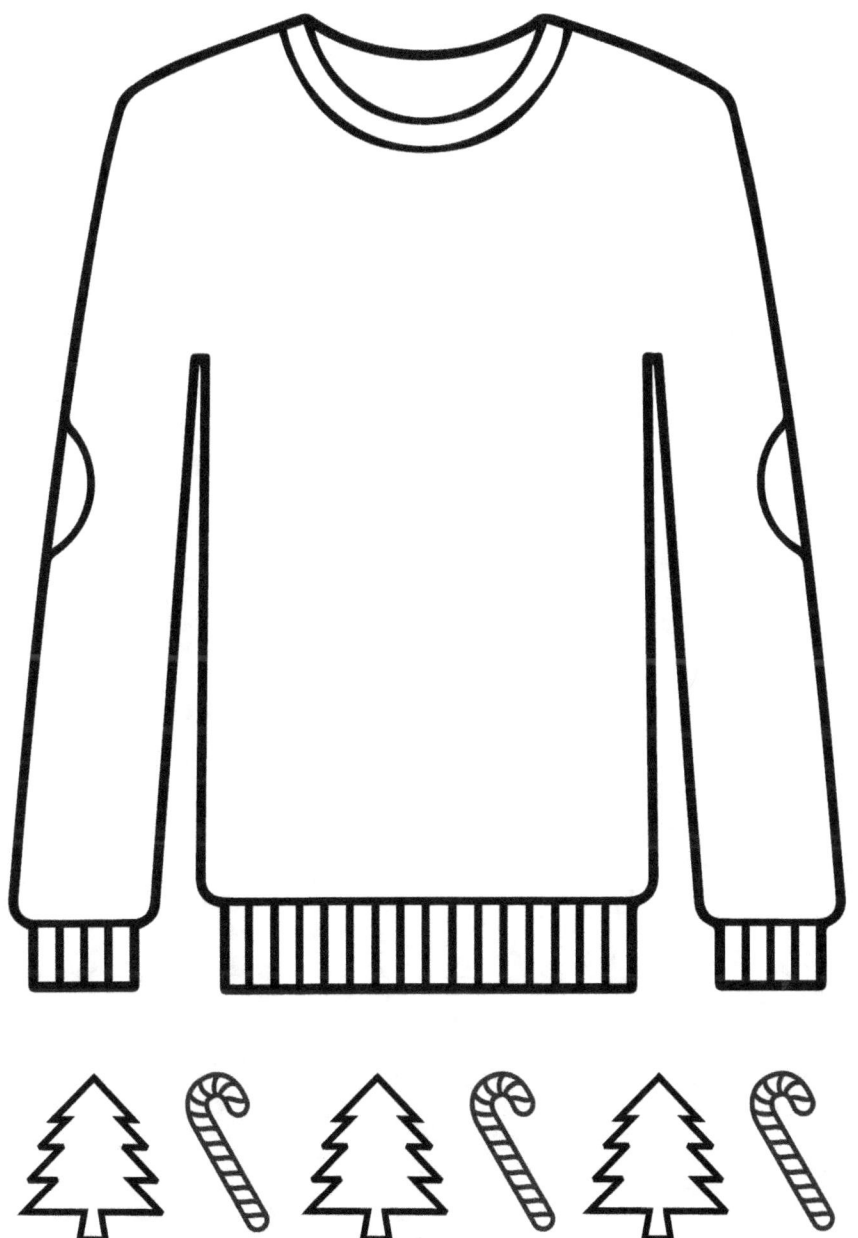

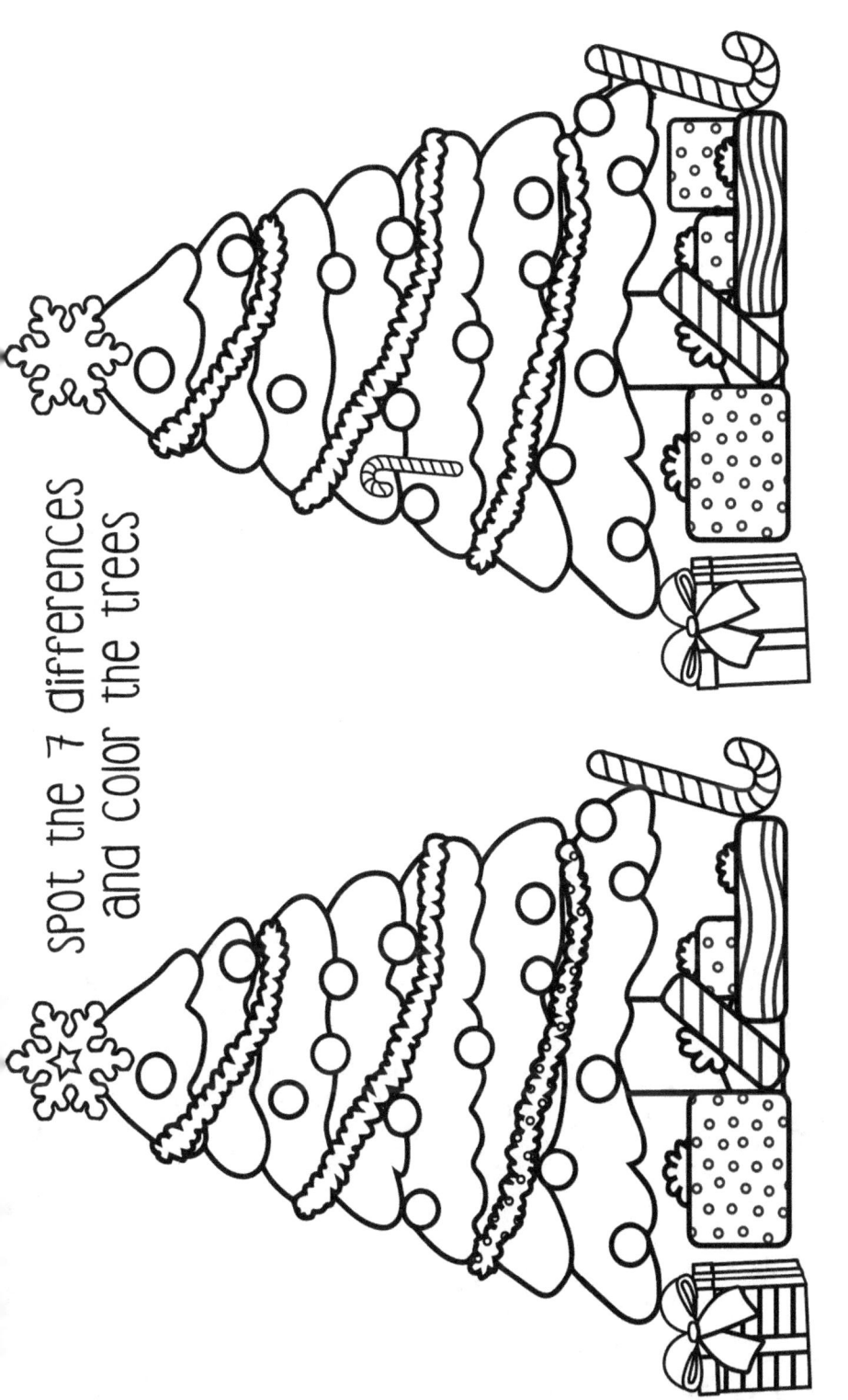

LEFT TREE HAS AN EXTRA ORNAMENT...MISSING STRIPE ON LEFT PRESENT
NO STAR ON THE RIGHT SNOWFLAKE...CANDY CANE IN RIGHT TREE
POLKA DOTS ON LEFT GARLAND...STRIPES ON LEFT PRESENT...EXTRA PRESENT ON RIGHT

SNOWMAN	**STOCKING**
CHRISTMAS TREE	**PRESENT**

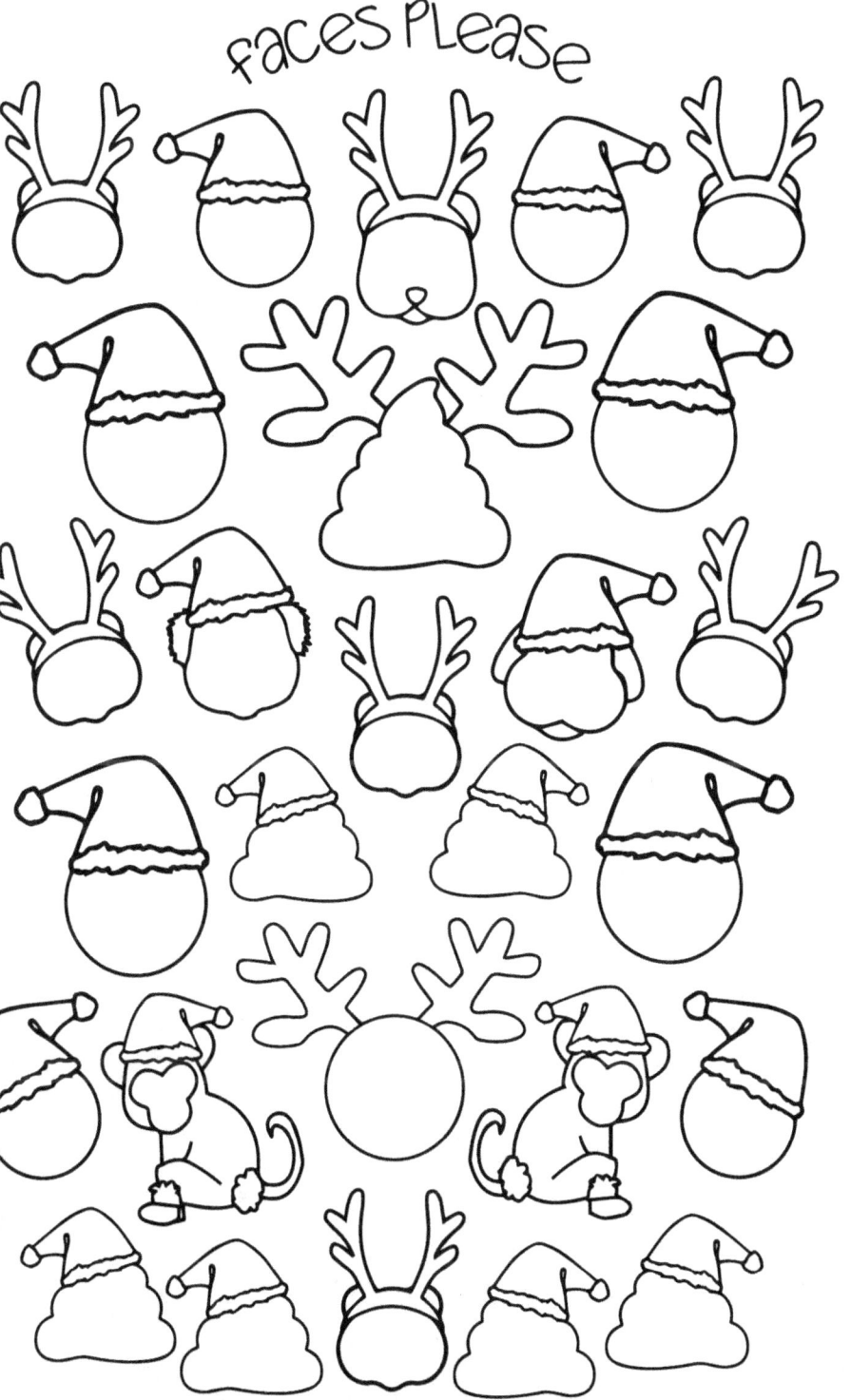

Design and color a Christmas Cake!

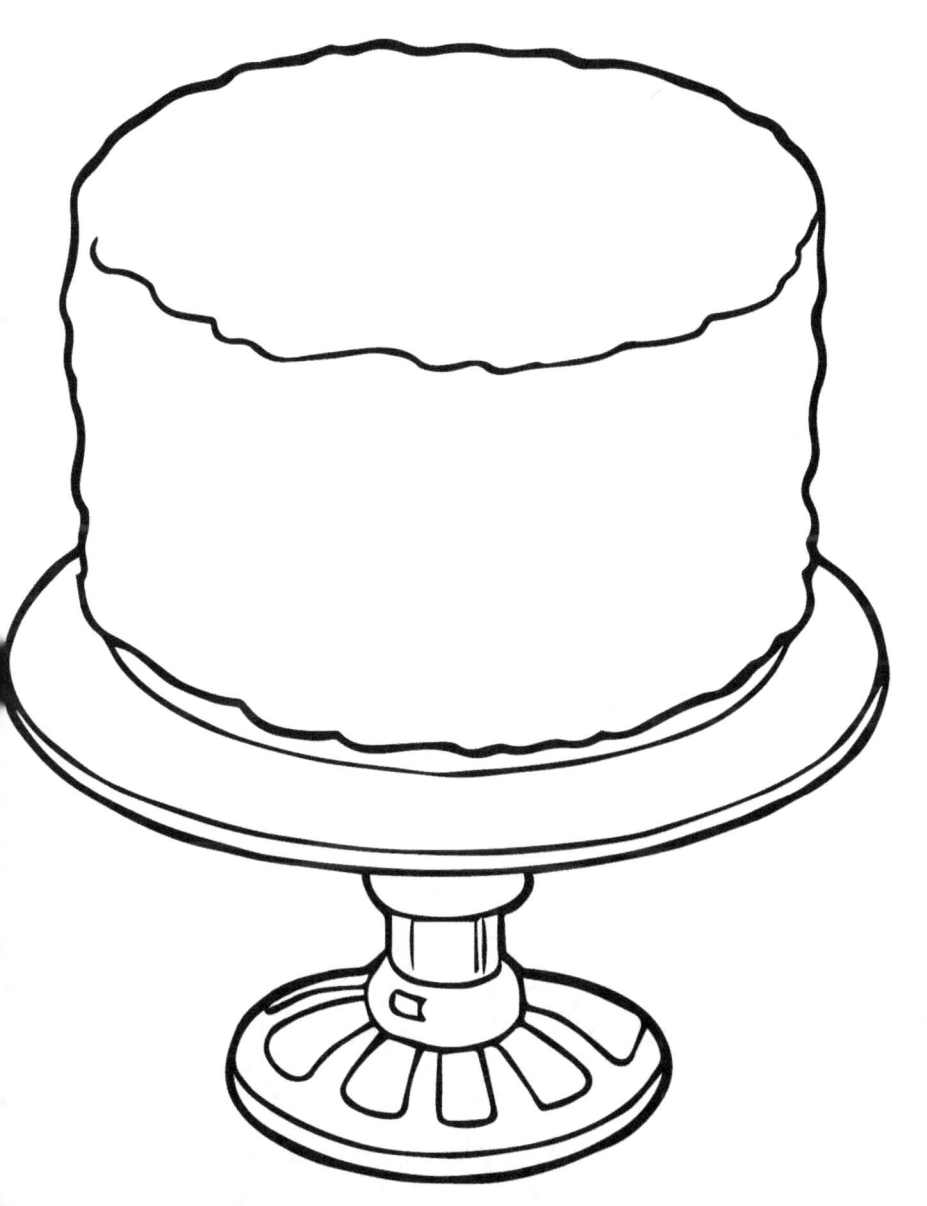

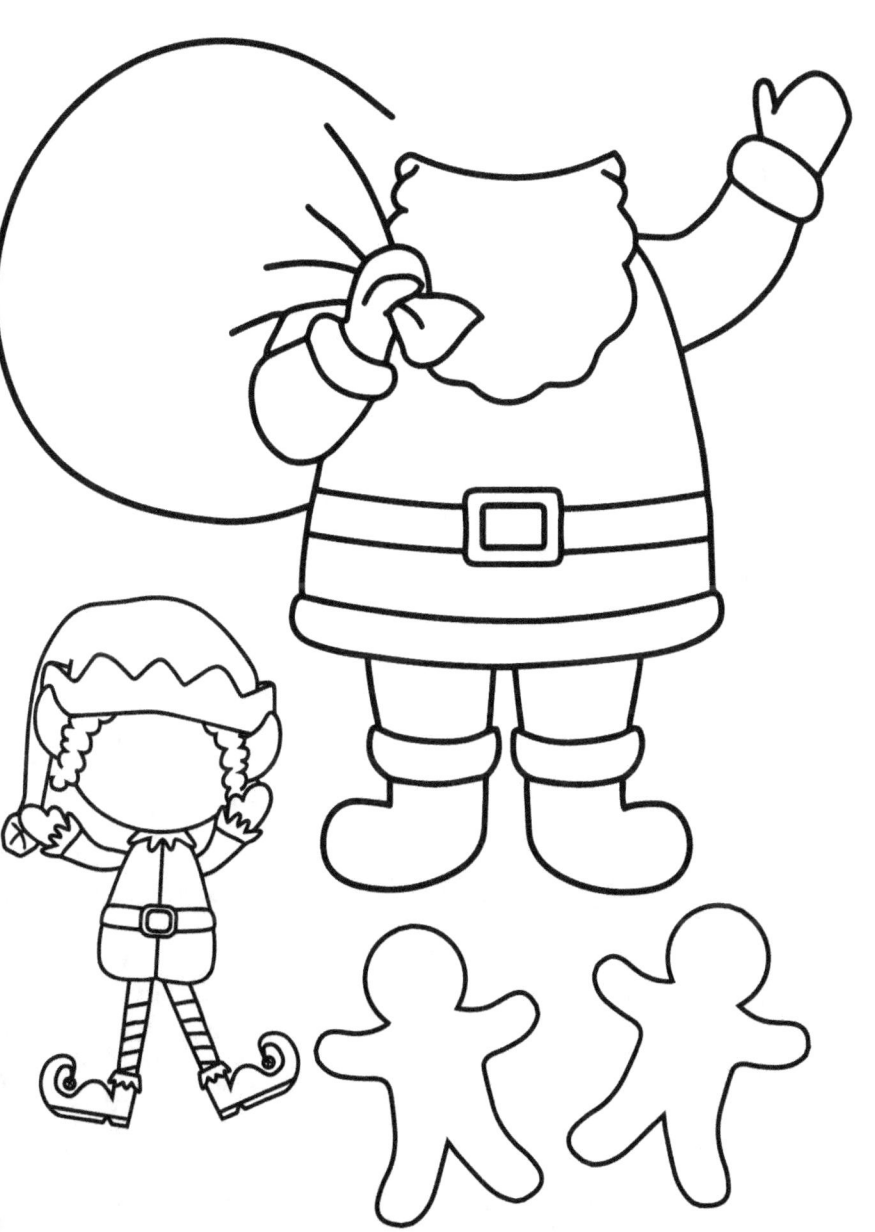

Word Scramble!

1. DNOREWADNL _____
2. ESCROGO _____
3. ASNAT LACSU _____
4. LLSEB _____
5. TEESRNSP _____
6. UHRDPLO _____
7. MASHCRIST EERT _____
8. ENOL _____
9. WNMOSAN _____
10. NDYCA ANCE _____
11. YOLLH _____
12. NIRGHC _____
13. ITSGF _____
14. EMRYR _____
15. TWARHE _____

1. WONDERLAND
2. SCROOGE
3. SANTA CLAUS
4. BELLS
5. PRESENTS
6. RUDOLPH
7. CHRISTMAS TREE
8. NOEL
9. SNOWMAN
10. CANDY CANE
11. HOLLY
12. GRINCH
13. GIFTS
14. MERRY
15. WREATH

YOU'RE GIVING OUT CHRISTMAS GIFTS!
WHO ARE THEY FOR?
DESIGN SOME NICE CHRISTMAS WRAPPING PAPER.

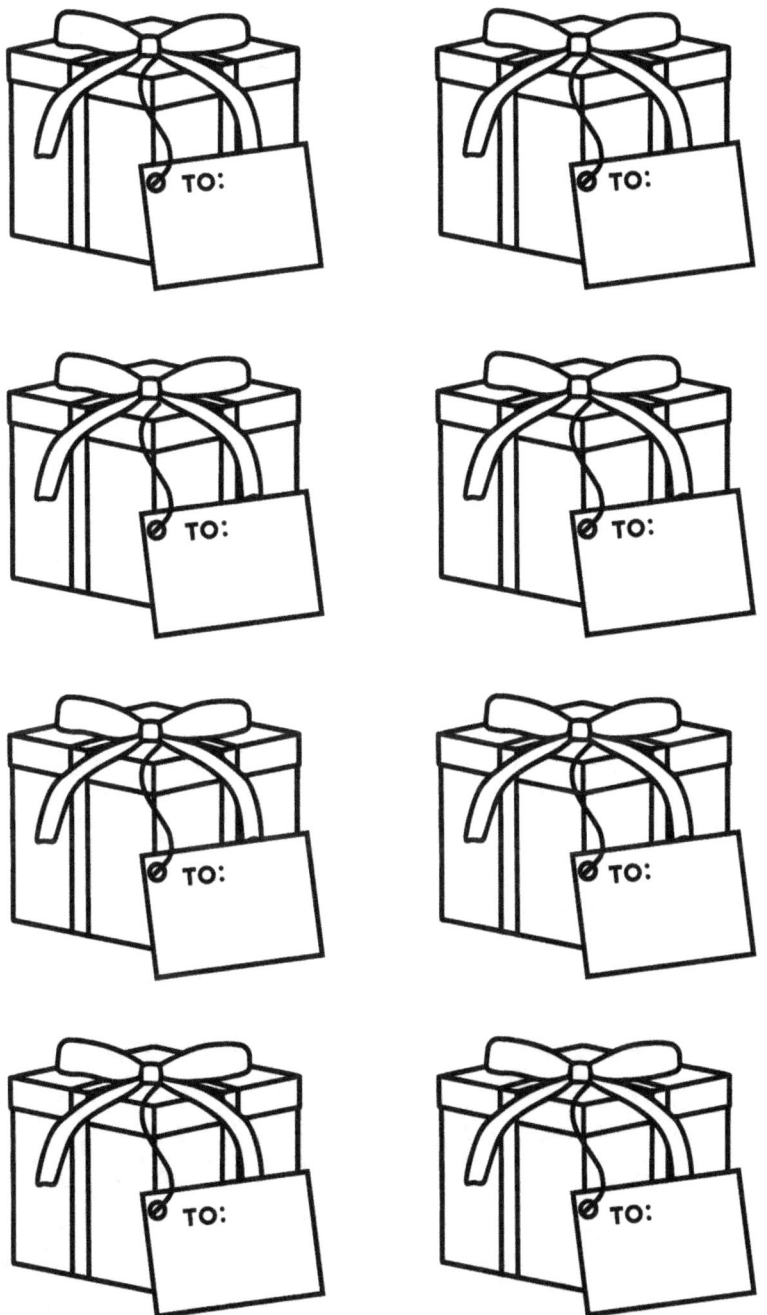

Design christmas ice skates

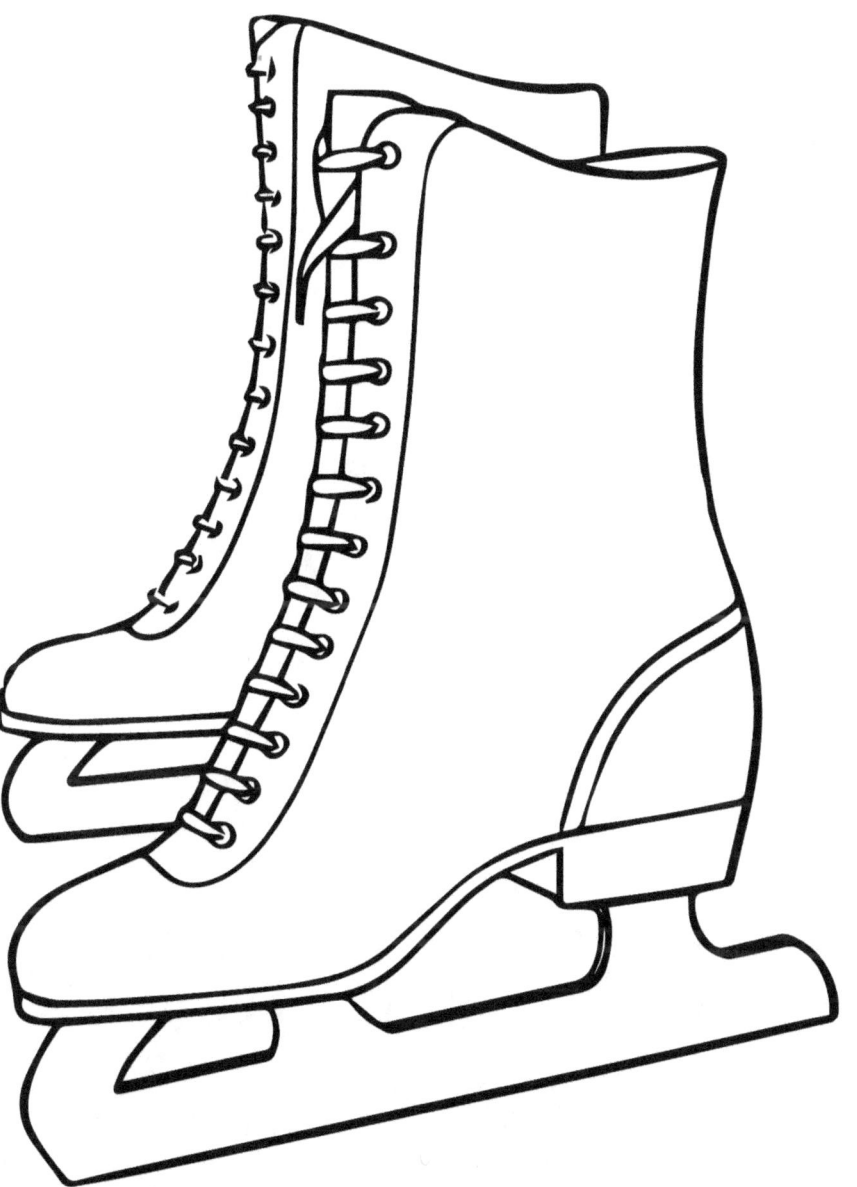

I'm thankful for:

1. _____
2. _____
3. _____
4. _____
5. _____
6. _____
7. _____
8. _____
9. _____
10. _____

www.ingramcontent.com/pod-product-compliance
Lightning Source LLC
Chambersburg PA
CBHW071420220526
45469CB00004B/1355